"There is nothing so American as our National Parks."

- Franklin D. Roosevelt

Designed and Illustrated by
JESSE BALMER

Research and text by
SAMUEL STEVENS
and
DYLAN BALMER

Published By
FLATLANDER TRADING

July 2023 | Des Moines, IA

THE STORY

The intial coneptualization of *Your Passport to the Parks* was birthed out of a friendship and a roadtrip. Fitting, right?

Sam and I often spoke about our love for travelling, visting the U.S. national parks, and photography. It didn't take us long to realize that we also had a shared desire to spend our time on the things that really matter in life.

Simply put, we wanted live life engaged. All in. Fully in the moment. We feared mindlessly watching the world move past while glued to the screen of our digital camera, iPhone, or the wrapped up in the thought of what photos we could share on social media. We didn't want to feel obligated to commemorate our trip through tacky gift shop t-shirts or another poorly designed postcard. After all, there are only so many shirts you can own and postcards that you can have on a fridge. We wanted to live life differently, and to help others do the same. If we were going to pour our energy into developing a new product, we wanted to be sure that it would be much more meaningful. We wanted to create a product that would allow someone to record the moments that really mattered; to document these moments in a simple, sophisticated, and beautiful way.

Your Passport to the Parks encourages travel, reflection, and intentionality. These principles are not only something that we want to foster through this travel journal but principles that we want to see worked into every area of our lives. The idea of living every moment with great intention drives the way we do life.

We sincerely hope *Your Passport to the Parks* is a joy to use and that it inspires you to document the moments that matter most.

- Jesse Balmer
  Author, Designer, and Creator of Your Passport to the Parks

Sam Stevens

Jesse Balmer

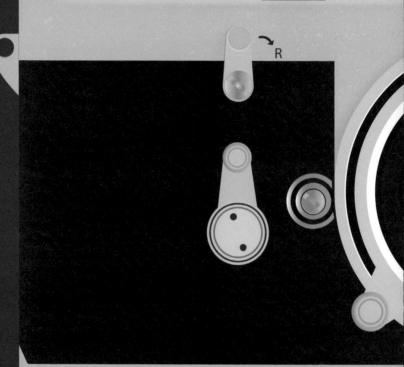

Eastern United States
PAGES 16 TO 33

Midwestern United States
PAGES 34 TO 55

Western United States
PAGES 56 TO 109

Southern United States
PAGES 110 TO 125

Hawaii & Alaska
PAGES 126 TO 147

Other U.S. Territories
PAGES 148 TO 153

THE PARKS OF THE EAST

18	ACADIA
20	BISCAYNE
22	CONGAREE
24	DRY TORTUGAS
26	EVERGLADES
28	GREAT SMOKY MOUNTAINS
30	NEW RIVER GORGE
32	SHENANDOAH

Parks

ACADIA | NP

Referred to as "The Crown Jewel of the North Atlantic Coast," Acadia National Park was federally recognized as the first national park east of the Mississippi River in 1919. Acadia National Park is located in northern Maine and is home to rocky shorelines, towering mountains, rich forests, beautiful hiking trails, and the all-encompassing Park Loop Road. Acadia National Park captures the splendor of the Northeast in more than 47,000 acres of coastal land, and it stands as one of the top 10 most visited national parks in the United States.

ACADIA NATIONAL PARK
NORTHERN MAINE

DATE

FIRST REACTION

TRAVEL COMPANIONS

WEATHER CONDITIONS

ACTIVITIES

MOST MEMORABLE MOMENT

RATING

CUPS OF COFFEE

PARK /63

MEMORABLE QUOTES

PARK STAMP

FAVORITE SPOT

DISTANCE TRAVELED

ADDITIONAL THOUGHTS

Parks

BISCAYNE | NP

Located just southeast of Miami, Florida, Biscayne National Park boasts the largest underwater ecosystem protected by the National Park Service. While there are many sights to see on the dry ground of the Biscayne Keys, 95 percent of this park lies underwater and accessible only by boat. Underwater, scuba divers and snorkelers have the opportunity to see several shipwrecks, coral reefs, and over 500 species of fish. Goggles and air tanks aren't for you? You are still able to experience the beauty of this national park by visiting Boca Chita Key or by taking a boat trip to see shipwrecks on the Maritime Heritage Trail.

BISCAYNE NATIONAL PARK
FLORIDA KEYS

DATE

FIRST REACTION

TRAVEL COMPANIONS

WEATHER CONDITIONS

ACTIVITIES

MOST MEMORABLE MOMENT

RATING

CUPS OF COFFEE

PARK /63

MEMORABLE QUOTES

PARK STAMP

FAVORITE SPOT

DISTANCE TRAVELED

ADDITIONAL THOUGHTS

Parks

CONGAREE | NP

Home to some of the oldest trees in America, Congaree National Park is comprised of 20,000 acres of hardwood forest. While this park doesn't draw in millions of visitors each year, it offers a diverse range of wildlife, 25 miles of trails, and so much to explore. Without an entrance fee, visiting Congaree National Park is a no-brainer. Stop by and check out the swamps and champion trees, even if just for a short visit. There's nothing quite like it.

CONGAREE NATIONAL PARK
SOUTH CAROLINA

DATE

FIRST REACTION

TRAVEL COMPANIONS

WEATHER CONDITIONS

ACTIVITIES

MOST MEMORABLE MOMENT

RATING

CUPS OF COFFEE

PARK /63

MEMORABLE QUOTES

PARK STAMP

FAVORITE SPOT

DISTANCE TRAVELED

ADDITIONAL THOUGHTS

Parks

DRY TORTUGAS | NP

Roughly 70 miles west of Florida's Key West lies Dry Tortugas National Park. Dry Tortugas is home to Fort Jefferson, a historic fort built for United States' defense in the gulf and later used as a prison during the Civil War. The beauty above ground in this national park pales in comparison to the underwater wonders that lie below. From the sprawling labyrinth of coral reefs to the nesting sea turtles, tropical fish, and one of North America's largest collections of shipwrecks, visiting Dry Tortugas National Park is sure to be an unforgettable experience.

DRY TORTUGAS NATIONAL PARK
FLORIDA KEYS

DATE

FIRST REACTION

TRAVEL COMPANIONS

WEATHER CONDITIONS

ACTIVITIES

MOST MEMORABLE MOMENT

RATING

CUPS OF COFFEE

PARK /63

MEMORABLE QUOTES

PARK STAMP

FAVORITE SPOT

DISTANCE TRAVELED

ADDITIONAL THOUGHTS

Parks

EVERGLADES | NP

Stretching along a 100-mile subtropical waterway of the southern tip of Florida, Everglades National Park is a unique ecosystem full of swamps, saw-grass prairie, and a large variety of wildlife. Among the many alligators you will find lurking in the swampy waters, you will find many species of unique plants and birds. Consider walking along a self-guided walkway through this jungle-like environment, or even canoe through some of the waterways to get a closer look!

EVERGLADES NATIONAL PARK
SOUTHERN FLORIDA

DATE

FIRST REACTION

TRAVEL COMPANIONS

WEATHER CONDITIONS

ACTIVITIES

MOST MEMORABLE MOMENT

RATING

CUPS OF COFFEE

PARK
/63

MEMORABLE QUOTES

PARK STAMP

FAVORITE SPOT

DISTANCE TRAVELED

ADDITIONAL THOUGHTS

Parks

GREAT SMOKY MOUNTAINS | NP

Claiming the coveted title of the most visited national park, Great Smoky Mountains National Park draws over 14 million visitors each and every year. In addition to being a highly visited national park, Great Smoky Mountains National Park is also the most biodiverse national park - containing a whopping 19,000 documented species of plants, animals, and other organisms. Visitors can expect to find an abundance of hiking trails, waterfalls, and mountain-top views and can often view the valleys covered in a thick blanket of clouds - a particularly beautiful sight when seen from above.

GREAT SMOKY MOUNTAINS NATIONAL PARK
NORTH CAROLINA

DATE

FIRST REACTION

TRAVEL COMPANIONS

WEATHER CONDITIONS

ACTIVITIES

MOST MEMORABLE MOMENT

RATING

CUPS OF COFFEE

PARK   /63

MEMORABLE QUOTES

PARK STAMP

FAVORITE SPOT

DISTANCE TRAVELED

ADDITIONAL THOUGHTS

Parks

NEW RIVER GORGE | NP

New River Gorge National Park and Preserve follows the New River for approximately 53 miles in West Virginia and became recognized as a national park in 2019. This park is a hotbed for extreme sports such as rock climbing, white-water rafting, and even base jumping. However, the casual visitor can hike numerous trails or take pictures at various scenic overlooks. The Canyon Rim Visitor Center and Grandview Visitor Center are two great places to start your journey!

NEW RIVER GORGE NATIONAL PARK
WEST VIRGINIA

DATE

FIRST REACTION

TRAVEL COMPANIONS

WEATHER CONDITIONS

ACTIVITIES

MOST MEMORABLE MOMENT

RATING

CUPS OF COFFEE

PARK /63

MEMORABLE QUOTES

PARK STAMP

FAVORITE SPOT

DISTANCE TRAVELED

ADDITIONAL THOUGHTS

Parks

SHENANDOAH | NP

The 105-mile-long Skyline Drive that winds upon Virginia's Appalachian Mountains is a true gem of the East Coast - and it's just Shenandoah National Park's icing on the cake. Beyond Skyline Drive lies 300 square miles of Appalachian wilderness full of black bears, waterfalls, wildflowers, and epic views of the Blue Ridge Mountains. Whether by car or by foot, time spent traversing the beautiful landscape of Shenandoah National Park is time well spent.

SHENANDOAH NATIONAL PARK
VIRGINIA

DATE

FIRST REACTION

TRAVEL COMPANIONS

WEATHER CONDITIONS

ACTIVITIES

MOST MEMORABLE MOMENT

RATING
🌲 🌲 🌲 🌲 🌲

CUPS OF COFFEE
☕ ☕ ☕ ☕ ☕

PARK
/63

MEMORABLE QUOTES

PARK STAMP

FAVORITE SPOT

DISTANCE TRAVELED

ADDITIONAL THOUGHTS

36	BADLANDS
38	CUYAHOGA VALLEY
40	GATEWAY ARCH
42	HOT SPRINGS
44	INDIANA DUNES
46	ISLE ROYALE
48	MAMMOTH CAVES
50	THEODORE ROOSEVELT
52	VOYAGEURS
54	WIND CAVE

Parks

BADLANDS | NP

Like many of our nation's national parks, Badlands National Park could be described as other-worldly. Highway 240 takes visitors on a 40-mile drive straight through the national park from Interior, SD, to Wall, SD (home of Wall Drug). We promise that this park will make you feel like you are on another planet! Be sure to get out of the car and walk around or climb the badlands to get a grasp of the scope of these geological formations. While most visitors never leave the badland portion of the park, Badlands National Park extends far beyond Highway 240 and has thousands of acres of protected prairie where sheep and buffalo can be spotted.

BADLANDS NATIONAL PARK
SOUTH DAKOTA

DATE | FIRST REACTION

TRAVEL COMPANIONS

WEATHER CONDITIONS

ACTIVITIES

MOST MEMORABLE MOMENT

RATING | CUPS OF COFFEE | PARK /63

MEMORABLE QUOTES | PARK STAMP

FAVORITE SPOT

DISTANCE TRAVELED

ADDITIONAL THOUGHTS

Parks

CUYAHOGA VALLEY | NP

Located between Cleveland and Akron, Ohio, Cuyahoga Valley National Park follows the Cuyahoga River and is flanked by suburban neighborhoods, a ski hill, and golf courses. Partly due to its location in a highly-populated area, this park boasts an annual guest count of over 2.2 million visitors. Waterfalls, the scenic railway, bike trails, and hiking trails offer an escape from the hustle and bustle of city life.

CUYAHOGA VALLEY NATIONAL PARK
NORTHEASTERN OHIO

DATE

FIRST REACTION

TRAVEL COMPANIONS

WEATHER CONDITIONS

ACTIVITIES

MOST MEMORABLE MOMENT

RATING

CUPS OF COFFEE

PARK /63

MEMORABLE QUOTES

PARK STAMP

FAVORITE SPOT

DISTANCE TRAVELED

ADDITIONAL THOUGHTS

Parks

GATEWAY ARCH | NP

Gateway Arch National Park holds two iconic pieces of American history: the 630-foot stainless steel arch and the Old Courthouse of St. Louis. The design for the Gateway Arch that now stands is the winning design from a competition to create a national monument to commemorate the westward expansion of the 19th century. Visitors can peer up at the monstrous size of the arch, take a tram to the top, visit the museum below, or tour the Old Courthouse.

GATEWAY ARCH NATIONAL PARK
ST. LOUIS, MISSOURI

DATE

FIRST REACTION

TRAVEL COMPANIONS

WEATHER CONDITIONS

ACTIVITIES

MOST MEMORABLE MOMENT

RATING

CUPS OF COFFEE

PARK /63

MEMORABLE QUOTES

PARK STAMP

FAVORITE SPOT

DISTANCE TRAVELED

ADDITIONAL THOUGHTS

Parks

HOT SPRINGS | NP

At the base of Hot Springs Mountain in central Arkansas lies the beautiful Hot Springs National Park. Out of these hot springs flow a half-million gallons of water each day - giving life to the infamous "BathHouse Row" and the surrounding landscape. Visitors can, to this day, enjoy a bath in the waters of these hot springs by visiting the Buckstaff Baths and can see the 40 natural hot springs via 20+ miles of hiking trails.

HOT SPRINGS NATIONAL PARK
CENTRAL ARKANSAS

DATE

FIRST REACTION

TRAVEL COMPANIONS

WEATHER CONDITIONS

ACTIVITIES

MOST MEMORABLE MOMENT

RATING

CUPS OF COFFEE

PARK /63

MEMORABLE QUOTES

PARK STAMP

FAVORITE SPOT

DISTANCE TRAVELED

ADDITIONAL THOUGHTS

Parks

INDIANA DUNES | NP

At the southern tip of Lake Michigan lies the 61st United States National Park - Indiana Dunes National Park. This park covers more than 20 miles of Lake Michigan shoreline and is known for its sand dunes and its large number of biking and hiking trails. Consider taking on the "3 Dune Challenge" - conquering three dunes and 557 vertical feet over the course of 1.5 miles or just soaking in some summer sun on the beautiful shoreline. On a clear day, you may even catch a glimpse of the Chicago skyline.

INDIANA DUNES NATIONAL PARK
NORTHERN INDIANA

DATE

FIRST REACTION

TRAVEL COMPANIONS

WEATHER CONDITIONS

ACTIVITIES

MOST MEMORABLE MOMENT

RATING

CUPS OF COFFEE

PARK /63

MEMORABLE QUOTES

PARK STAMP

FAVORITE SPOT

DISTANCE TRAVELED

ADDITIONAL THOUGHTS

Parks

ISLE ROYALE | NP

Located 56 miles off the coast of Michigan and completely surrounded by the waters of Lake Superior, Isle Royale National Park is exclusively accessible by ferry or seaplane. Over 165 miles of hiking trails allow hikers to travel deep into this remote wilderness, and visitors often leave feeling refreshed by Isle Royale's tranquil environment. Keep your eyes peeled – it is not uncommon to catch a glimpse of a moose or wolf on your visit.

ISLE ROYALE NATIONAL PARK
NORTHERN MICHIGAN

DATE

FIRST REACTION

TRAVEL COMPANIONS

WEATHER CONDITIONS

ACTIVITIES

MOST MEMORABLE MOMENT

RATING

CUPS OF COFFEE

PARK   / 63

MEMORABLE QUOTES

PARK STAMP

FAVORITE SPOT

DISTANCE TRAVELED

ADDITIONAL THOUGHTS

Parks

MAMMOTH CAVE | NP

While this national park hosts over 400 miles of caves, including its namesake "Mammoth Cave," Mammoth Cave National Park also has much to offer above ground. This park features 85 miles of trails for biking and hiking and 30 miles of scenic waterways. For those eager to explore the Mammoth Cave, 12 cave routes are available to match interests and physical abilities. Before your visit, be sure to purchase your tickets through www.recreation.gov, as cave tour tickets often sell out quickly.

MAMMOTH CAVE NATIONAL PARK
SOUTHWESTERN KENTUCKY

DATE

FIRST REACTION

TRAVEL COMPANIONS

WEATHER CONDITIONS

ACTIVITIES

MOST MEMORABLE MOMENT

RATING

CUPS OF COFFEE

PARK /63

MEMORABLE QUOTES

PARK STAMP

FAVORITE SPOT

DISTANCE TRAVELED

ADDITIONAL THOUGHTS

Parks

THEODORE ROOSEVELT | NP

Theodore Roosevelt National Park, located in western North Dakota, is known to be the place where President Theodore Roosevelt fell in love with the Western United States years before he entered public office. To this day, Theodore Roosevelt National Park remains a beautiful wilderness of colorful badlands full of Great Plains wildlife. This landscape remains a rugged and beautiful destination for camping and hiking - as summers in the National Park are modest in temperature.

THEODORE ROOSEVELT NATIONAL PARK
NORTH DAKOTA

DATE

FIRST REACTION

TRAVEL COMPANIONS

WEATHER CONDITIONS

ACTIVITIES

MOST MEMORABLE MOMENT

RATING

CUPS OF COFFEE

PARK /63

MEMORABLE QUOTES

PARK STAMP

FAVORITE SPOT

DISTANCE TRAVELED

ADDITIONAL THOUGHTS

Parks

VOYAGEURS | NP

Hidden waterfalls, petroglyphs, lakes, and 25 miles of hiking trails are just a few things that make Voyageurs National Park unlike anywhere else. This national park, located near the Minnesota - Canada border, is only accessible by boat for most of the year but can be accessed by snowmobile when ice packs are fully formed. Summer months bring many campers, hikers, kayakers, and fishermen to the national park, but winter months offer a whole new set of opportunities to cross country ski, snowmobile, snowshoe, and even drive vehicles onto the frozen lakes to ice fish.

VOYAGEURS NATIONAL PARK
NORTHERN MINNESOTA

DATE

FIRST REACTION

TRAVEL COMPANIONS

WEATHER CONDITIONS

ACTIVITIES

MOST MEMORABLE MOMENT

RATING

CUPS OF COFFEE

PARK   /63

MEMORABLE QUOTES

PARK STAMP

FAVORITE SPOT

DISTANCE TRAVELED

ADDITIONAL THOUGHTS

Parks

WIND CAVE | NP

Nestled in the Black Hills and often forgotten in the shadow of Mt. Rushmore, Wind Cave National Park is a 150-mile-long cave situated 500 feet underneath the South Dakota prairie land. Unfortunately, most of the caves are inaccessible to the general public, but guided tours from the visitor center are available on a daily basis. For those who do not want to venture into the caves, hiking trails across the prairie are available where visitors can spot bison, coyotes, pronghorns, and, on rare occasions, elk.

WIND CAVE NATIONAL PARK
SOUTH DAKOTA

DATE

FIRST REACTION

TRAVEL COMPANIONS

WEATHER CONDITIONS

ACTIVITIES

MOST MEMORABLE MOMENT

RATING

CUPS OF COFFEE

PARK
/63

MEMORABLE QUOTES

PARK STAMP

FAVORITE SPOT

DISTANCE TRAVELED

ADDITIONAL THOUGHTS

58	ARCHES
60	BLACK CANYON OF THE GUNNISON
62	BRYCE CANYON
64	CANYONLANDS
66	CAPITOL REEF
68	CHANNEL ISLANDS
70	CRATER LAKE
72	DEATH VALLEY
74	GLACIER
76	GRAND TETON
78	GREAT BASIN
80	GREAT SAND DUNES
82	JOSHUA TREE
84	KINGS CANYON
86	LASSEN VOLCANIC
88	MESA VERDE
90	MT. RAINIER
92	NORTH CASCADES
94	OLYMPIC
96	PINNACLES
98	REDWOODS
100	ROCKY MOUNTAIN
102	SEQUOIA
104	YELLOWSTONE
106	YOSEMITE
108	ZION

Parks

ARCHES | NP

One of Utah's "Mighty 5", Arches National Park is famous for its high concentration of natural sandstone arches. Delicate Arch and the Double Arch are the most famous of these sandstone formations. Natural erosion created these arches over time, and, with more time, could destroy them. With that being said, be sure to take the chance to visit this park, whether it's via the 18-mile scenic drive, a 5-hour hike, or a day of rock climbing!

ARCHES NATIONAL PARK
SOUTHERN UTAH

DATE

FIRST REACTION

TRAVEL COMPANIONS

WEATHER CONDITIONS

ACTIVITIES

MOST MEMORABLE MOMENT

RATING

CUPS OF COFFEE

PARK /63

MEMORABLE QUOTES

PARK STAMP

FAVORITE SPOT

DISTANCE TRAVELED

ADDITIONAL THOUGHTS

Parks

BLACK CANYON OF THE GUNNISON
NATIONAL PARK

Black Canyon of the Gunnison National Park showcases a variety of sharp black cliffs, crags, spires, and canyons deep within the heart of Colorado. The Gunnison River carved the abundance of advanced rock climbing, hiking, and kayaking opportunities into this park, and you can still see it sweeping through this canyon today. Consider hiking the Rim Rock Nature Trail or viewing this national park from the river via the Morrow Point Boat Tour.

BLACK CANYON OF THE GUNNISON NATIONAL PARK
WESTERN COLORADO

DATE

FIRST REACTION

TRAVEL COMPANIONS

WEATHER CONDITIONS

ACTIVITIES

MOST MEMORABLE MOMENT

RATING

CUPS OF COFFEE

PARK /63

MEMORABLE QUOTES

PARK STAMP

FAVORITE SPOT

DISTANCE TRAVELED

ADDITIONAL THOUGHTS

Parks

BRYCE CANYON | NP

Bryce Canyon National Park hosts incredible views brought to you by its sky-scraping rock fixtures - making it a truly enrapturing wonder. This national park has the largest concentration of irregular rock columns, or "hoodoos," on earth. Natural amphitheaters, canyons, points, spires, and plateaus are easily viewable from hiking trails or scenic roadways. Bring some hiking shoes - you'll want to experience all the geological beauty Bryce Canyon National Park offers up close.

BRYCE CANYON NATIONAL PARK
SOUTHERN UTAH

DATE

FIRST REACTION

TRAVEL COMPANIONS

WEATHER CONDITIONS

ACTIVITIES

MOST MEMORABLE MOMENT

RATING

CUPS OF COFFEE

PARK   /63

MEMORABLE QUOTES

PARK STAMP

FAVORITE SPOT

DISTANCE TRAVELED

ADDITIONAL THOUGHTS

Parks

CANYONLANDS | NP

Located in southeastern Utah, Canyonlands National Park sports breathtaking views carved by the Colorado River. The desertous environment of this national park is filled with a variety of rock formations that provide opportunities for hiking, sightseeing, and even white-water rafting. Many highly recommend visiting the Mesa Arch at sunrise to get the most picturesque view of this park.

CANYONLANDS NATIONAL PARK
SOUTHERN UTAH

DATE

FIRST REACTION

TRAVEL COMPANIONS

WEATHER CONDITIONS

ACTIVITIES

MOST MEMORABLE MOMENT

RATING

CUPS OF COFFEE

PARK /63

MEMORABLE QUOTES

PARK STAMP

FAVORITE SPOT

DISTANCE TRAVELED

ADDITIONAL THOUGHTS

Parks

CAPITOL REEF | NP

Capitol Reef National Park, located deep in the south-central region of Utah, is a park overflowing with geological beauty. The colorful sandstone monoliths, domes, canyons, and natural arches make this national park an oasis for any outdoor enthusiast. While visiting Capitol Reef National Park, be sure and visit the towering monoliths of the Cathedral Valley and the iconic Chimney Rock. Come prepared with some good hiking equipment - you won't want to miss out on anything this park has to offer.

CAPITOL REEF NATIONAL PARK
SOUTHERN UTAH

DATE

FIRST REACTION

TRAVEL COMPANIONS

WEATHER CONDITIONS

ACTIVITIES

MOST MEMORABLE MOMENT

RATING

CUPS OF COFFEE

PARK   /63

MEMORABLE QUOTES

PARK STAMP

FAVORITE SPOT

DISTANCE TRAVELED

ADDITIONAL THOUGHTS

Parks

CHANNEL ISLANDS | NP

Channel Islands National Park consists of five separate islands located along the coast of California. These islands are gorgeous sights in and of themselves and are also home to diverse plant and animal species. Channel Islands National Park has long been a refuge for marine life and is also a critical site for research on endangered species and conservation. Take some time to hike, whale watch, kayak, or even camp in this unique National Park. Don't forget to stay on marked trails and leave the protected plants and animals undisturbed.

CHANNEL ISLANDS NATIONAL PARK
CALIFORNIA

DATE

FIRST REACTION

TRAVEL COMPANIONS

WEATHER CONDITIONS

ACTIVITIES

MOST MEMORABLE MOMENT

RATING

CUPS OF COFFEE

PARK
/ 63

MEMORABLE QUOTES

PARK STAMP

FAVORITE SPOT

DISTANCE TRAVELED

ADDITIONAL THOUGHTS

Parks

CRATER LAKE | NP

Crater Lake is the deepest lake in the United States, boasting a maximum depth of 1,949 feet. This lake was created over 7,700 years ago due to a volcanic eruption and became designated as Crater Lake National Park in 1902. Much of this national park can be viewed from a scenic drive around the crater via the east/west rim drive. However, you won't regret taking time to hike the Watchman Peak Trail, taking a dip into the lake's chilly waters, or even taking a boat tour to Wizard Island.

CRATER LAKE NATIONAL PARK
SOUTHERN OREGON

DATE

FIRST REACTION

TRAVEL COMPANIONS

WEATHER CONDITIONS

ACTIVITIES

MOST MEMORABLE MOMENT

RATING

CUPS OF COFFEE

PARK   /63

MEMORABLE QUOTES

PARK STAMP

FAVORITE SPOT

DISTANCE TRAVELED

ADDITIONAL THOUGHTS

Parks

DEATH VALLEY | NP

Death Valley National Park is located 2 hours west of Las Vegas, Nevada, and can reach temperatures north of 130 degrees in the summer months. As you might guess, taking hikes for longer than 15 minutes is not recommended. Though this scorching landscape can be hostile to humans, this national park still has a thriving wildlife population, including bighorn sheep, jackrabbits, desert tortoises, and coyotes. While visiting, check out the salt flats of Badwater Basin, the lowest elevation in North America.

DEATH VALLEY NATIONAL PARK
EASTERN CALIFORNIA

DATE

FIRST REACTION

TRAVEL COMPANIONS

WEATHER CONDITIONS

ACTIVITIES

MOST MEMORABLE MOMENT

RATING

CUPS OF COFFEE

PARK
/63

MEMORABLE QUOTES

PARK STAMP

FAVORITE SPOT

DISTANCE TRAVELED

ADDITIONAL THOUGHTS

Parks

GLACIER | NP

While driving a 4x4 grants you access to even more remote mountain lakes and glaciers, Glacier National Park can be appreciated without going off-road. Going to The Sun Road is a perfect example of that! This road takes visitors across the middle of Glacier National Park, starting at Lake McDonald, crossing the continental divide at Logan Pass, and ending at Saint Mary Lake. This 50-mile road takes about two hours to drive and changes over 5,000 feet in elevation. Along the drive, there are many waterfalls, viewpoints, and lakes to hike to for various ability levels.

GLACIER NATIONAL PARK
NORTHWESTERN MONTANA

DATE

FIRST REACTION

TRAVEL COMPANIONS

WEATHER CONDITIONS

ACTIVITIES

MOST MEMORABLE MOMENT

RATING

CUPS OF COFFEE

PARK /63

MEMORABLE QUOTES

PARK STAMP

FAVORITE SPOT

DISTANCE TRAVELED

ADDITIONAL THOUGHTS

Parks

GRAND TETON | NP

Tucked away just a few miles north of Jackson, Wyoming, the mountains of Grand Teton National Park dominate the landscape. The Tetons are one of the grandest formations along the whole Rocky Mountain Range. These peaks reach heights over 14,000 feet. and stretch 7,000 feet above the valley floor below. Consider taking a day hike up into the mountains or canoeing on Jenny Lake at sunrise. You will most definitely be refreshed from the quiet and peaceful perspective of the mountain peaks from the crystal-clear waters.

GRAND TETON NATIONAL PARK
WESTERN WYOMING

DATE

FIRST REACTION

TRAVEL COMPANIONS

WEATHER CONDITIONS

ACTIVITIES

MOST MEMORABLE MOMENT

RATING

CUPS OF COFFEE

PARK /63

MEMORABLE QUOTES

PARK STAMP

FAVORITE SPOT

DISTANCE TRAVELED

ADDITIONAL THOUGHTS

Parks

GREAT BASIN | NP

Great Basin National Park is located in eastern Nevada, and while you may assume this region is nothing but a desert wilderness, Great Basin is a park of extremes. This national park's towering mountain peaks and sprawling cave systems stand in great contrast with one another. Popular attractions include spelunking the Lehman Caves, driving the Scenic Route, and climbing Wheeler's Peak to 13,065 feet. You won't want to miss out on all the adventures to be had at this national park!

GREAT BASIN NATIONAL PARK
EASTERN NEVADA

DATE

FIRST REACTION

TRAVEL COMPANIONS

WEATHER CONDITIONS

ACTIVITIES

MOST MEMORABLE MOMENT

RATING

CUPS OF COFFEE

PARK /63

MEMORABLE QUOTES

PARK STAMP

FAVORITE SPOT

DISTANCE TRAVELED

ADDITIONAL THOUGHTS

Parks

GREAT SAND DUNES | NP

Spanning 30 square miles and with mountains of sand as tall as 750 feet, Great Sand Dunes National Park is home to the largest sand dunes in North America. That's not all this national park offers; visitors will also find mountain peaks reaching heights of 13,000 ft., alpine lakes, forests, and wetlands. Popular activities include sandboarding or sledding down the dunes, hiking, and horseback riding. Don't leave your shoes in the car - sands reach temperatures as high as 150 degrees in the summer months.

GREAT SAND DUNES NATIONAL PARK
SOUTHERN COLORADO

DATE

FIRST REACTION

TRAVEL COMPANIONS

WEATHER CONDITIONS

ACTIVITIES

MOST MEMORABLE MOMENT

RATING

CUPS OF COFFEE

PARK /63

MEMORABLE QUOTES

PARK STAMP

FAVORITE SPOT

DISTANCE TRAVELED

ADDITIONAL THOUGHTS

Parks

JOSHUA TREE | NP

Well known for its namesake Joshua Tree Forest, Joshua Tree National Park is a vast desert wilderness comprised of dry lakes, sand dunes, rocky mountains, and flat valleys. Visitors can hike, bike, rock climb, or ride their horses throughout the park on over 300 miles of trails and 2,000+ climbing routes. Unique desert landscapes and a wide variety of activities regularly draw visitors from Los Angeles for day or weekend trips to escape the city.

JOSHUA TREE NATIONAL PARK
SOUTHERN CALIFORNIA

DATE

FIRST REACTION

TRAVEL COMPANIONS

WEATHER CONDITIONS

ACTIVITIES

MOST MEMORABLE MOMENT

RATING

CUPS OF COFFEE

PARK /63

MEMORABLE QUOTES

PARK STAMP

FAVORITE SPOT

DISTANCE TRAVELED

ADDITIONAL THOUGHTS

Parks

KINGS CANYON | NP

Deep in California's Sierra Nevada Mountains lies Kings Canyon National Park. From its sky-scraping groves of Sequoia trees to its rocky mountain peaks and lush valleys, Kings Canyon National Park is a perfect destination for any outdoor enthusiast. Kings Canyon National Park is jointly operated with Sequoia National Park and is easily accessible with the same visitor pass. If you are planning to spend a few days in Kings Canyon, consider backpacking the Rae Lakes Loop Trail and venturing into the beautiful backcountry of this national park.

KINGS CANYON NATIONAL PARK
CALIFORNIA

DATE

FIRST REACTION

TRAVEL COMPANIONS

WEATHER CONDITIONS

ACTIVITIES

MOST MEMORABLE MOMENT

RATING

CUPS OF COFFEE

PARK /63

MEMORABLE QUOTES

PARK STAMP

FAVORITE SPOT

DISTANCE TRAVELED

ADDITIONAL THOUGHTS

Parks

LASSEN VOLCANIC | NP

Lassen Volcanic National Park, located in northern California, is home to all four types of volcanoes, including the park's iconic Lassen Peak - the largest plug-dome volcano in the world. Visitors can see this volcanic activity in action by visiting the many mud pots, steam vents, and bubbling springs throughout the park. Consider hiking Lassen Peak to see its volcanic crater or walking through active geothermal zones via the Bumpass Hell Trail.

LASSEN VOLCANIC NATIONAL PARK
NORTHERN CALIFORNIA

DATE

FIRST REACTION

TRAVEL COMPANIONS

WEATHER CONDITIONS

ACTIVITIES

MOST MEMORABLE MOMENT

RATING

CUPS OF COFFEE

PARK /63

MEMORABLE QUOTES

PARK STAMP

FAVORITE SPOT

DISTANCE TRAVELED

ADDITIONAL THOUGHTS

Parks

MESA VERDE | NP

Situated near the four-corner intersection of Colorado, Utah, Arizona, and New Mexico, Mesa Verde National Park is full of the history of the indigenous Anasazi people. Thousands of prehistoric sites have been found in this national park, and many of the cliff dwellings and pueblos can be seen from park overlooks and are open to the public. Best of all, you can visit this park any time of year. Don't miss out on this opportunity to see such rich indiginous history preserved in rock.

MESA VERDE NATIONAL PARK
SOUTHWESTERN COLORADO

DATE

FIRST REACTION

TRAVEL COMPANIONS

WEATHER CONDITIONS

ACTIVITIES

MOST MEMORABLE MOMENT

RATING

CUPS OF COFFEE

PARK /63

MEMORABLE QUOTES

PARK STAMP

FAVORITE SPOT

DISTANCE TRAVELED

ADDITIONAL THOUGHTS

Parks

MT. RAINIER | NP

Visible from nearly 300 miles away on a clear day, stratovolcano Mount Rainier dominates the Washington landscape and its 14,410 ft. summit commands respect. As the name suggests, Mt. Rainier National Park centers around the park's stratovolcano, but the park offers so much more. Opportunities to see wildlife, glaciers, waterfalls, and lush forests barely scratch the surface. While the summit of Mt. Rainier is visible from many places around the park, the best view of the glacier-covered peak is from Paradise, unless you decide to take on the challenge of climbing this monstrous peak.

MT. RAINIER NATIONAL PARK
WASHINGTON

DATE

FIRST REACTION

TRAVEL COMPANIONS

WEATHER CONDITIONS

ACTIVITIES

MOST MEMORABLE MOMENT

RATING

CUPS OF COFFEE

PARK /63

MEMORABLE QUOTES

PARK STAMP

FAVORITE SPOT

DISTANCE TRAVELED

ADDITIONAL THOUGHTS

Parks

NORTH CASCADES | NP

Just a 3-hour journey north from Seattle, Washington, North Cascades National Park is not far out of reach. Unlike most national parks, the majority of North Cascades National Park can only be seen from trails - not the car. The 300 Glaciers, countless snow-capped mountains, alpine forests, waterfalls, and cotton-candy blue lakes make this national park a must-see destination. Due to its thriving wildlife population and the smaller number of annual visitors, extra trip preparation is recommended for those planning to do extensive exploring.

NORTH CASCADES NATIONAL PARK
NORTHERN WASHINGTON

DATE

FIRST REACTION

TRAVEL COMPANIONS

WEATHER CONDITIONS

ACTIVITIES

MOST MEMORABLE MOMENT

RATING

CUPS OF COFFEE

PARK /63

MEMORABLE QUOTES

PARK STAMP

FAVORITE SPOT

DISTANCE TRAVELED

ADDITIONAL THOUGHTS

Parks

OLYMPIC | NP

In the northwestern corner of the continental United States lies Olympic National Park. If there's one word to describe this park, it's most definitely "diverse." From its glacier-capped mountain peaks to its rainforests, hot springs, neon-blue rivers, and other-worldly coastlines, you won't want to make a quick trip to Olympic National Park. When visiting Olympic National Park, consider taking a couple of days to complete the Olympic Peninsula Loop to see as much of this diverse landscape as possible. You won't be disappointed!

OLYMPIC NATIONAL PARK
NORTHWESTERN WASHINGTON

DATE

FIRST REACTION

TRAVEL COMPANIONS

WEATHER CONDITIONS

ACTIVITIES

MOST MEMORABLE MOMENT

RATING

CUPS OF COFFEE

PARK / 63

MEMORABLE QUOTES

PARK STAMP

FAVORITE SPOT

DISTANCE TRAVELED

ADDITIONAL THOUGHTS

Parks

PINNACLES | NP

Birthed out of ancient volcanic activity, Pinnacles National Park in west-central California is known for its other-worldly rock formations. From its sprawling cave system to the sky-scraping monoliths of rock, this national park is sure to be unlike anything you have seen. Pinnacles National Park is a climber's paradise, but there are still many hiking trails and activities for those who like to stay on solid ground. Don't forget to watch for the 9-foot wing spanned California Condors that may circle above, as they are the largest North American land bird and happen to call Pinnacles National Park home.

PINNACLES NATIONAL PARK
CALIFORNIA

DATE

FIRST REACTION

TRAVEL COMPANIONS

WEATHER CONDITIONS

ACTIVITIES

MOST MEMORABLE MOMENT

RATING

CUPS OF COFFEE

PARK /63

MEMORABLE QUOTES

PARK STAMP

FAVORITE SPOT

DISTANCE TRAVELED

ADDITIONAL THOUGHTS

Parks

REDWOODS | NP

Redwood National Park lies along the Pacific coast in northwestern California. This national park is home to the world's largest tree, "Hyperion," which stands at a staggering 379 feet tall. For comparison, the Statue of Liberty is only 305 feet tall! Consider taking a 3.3-mile hike through the Tall Trees Grove, where you will find countless redwood trees that exceed 350 feet tall. No matter how tall you are, you will feel small when you walk next to these mammoth trees.

REDWOODS NATIONAL PARK
NORTHERN CALIFORNIA

DATE

FIRST REACTION

TRAVEL COMPANIONS

WEATHER CONDITIONS

ACTIVITIES

MOST MEMORABLE MOMENT

RATING

CUPS OF COFFEE

PARK /63

MEMORABLE QUOTES

PARK STAMP

FAVORITE SPOT

DISTANCE TRAVELED

ADDITIONAL THOUGHTS

Parks

ROCKY MOUNTAIN | NP

Located on the Continental Divide in northern Colorado lies one of the most famous of the United States national parks - Rocky Mountain National Park. With more than 100 Mountain Peaks above 11,000 ft, the highest paved highway in the United States, and countless mountain lakes nestled in the Estes Valley, Rocky Mountain National Park is a must-see for any traveler! This national park is open year-round and is most known for having a large variety of hiking opportunities. Whether you would like to walk a paved trail to Bear Lake or hike upwards of 16 miles to the top of Longs Peak, adventures both small and large await you!

ROCKY MOUNTAIN NATIONAL PARK
NORTHERN COLORADO

DATE

FIRST REACTION

TRAVEL COMPANIONS

WEATHER CONDITIONS

ACTIVITIES

MOST MEMORABLE MOMENT

RATING

CUPS OF COFFEE

PARK /63

MEMORABLE QUOTES

PARK STAMP

FAVORITE SPOT

DISTANCE TRAVELED

ADDITIONAL THOUGHTS

Parks

SEQUOIA | NP

Sequoia National Park is world-renowned for its giant sequoia trees, and rightfully so. Five of the world's ten largest trees dwell in the Giant Forest of Sequoia National Park. Eighty-four percent of this national park remains designated backcountry wilderness and is only accessible by foot or horseback. While you're visiting, check out Sequoia National Park's neighbor, Kings Canyon National Park. One entrance fee will grant you access to both national parks!

SEQUOIA NATIONAL PARK
CALIFORNIA

DATE

FIRST REACTION

TRAVEL COMPANIONS

WEATHER CONDITIONS

ACTIVITIES

MOST MEMORABLE MOMENT

RATING

CUPS OF COFFEE

PARK /63

MEMORABLE QUOTES

PARK STAMP

FAVORITE SPOT

DISTANCE TRAVELED

ADDITIONAL THOUGHTS

Parks

YELLOWSTONE | NP

Yellowstone National Park is the first established United States national park and may be the most famous of them all. Since 1872, visitors have trekked to this national park to see its strange geological features and to experience the wonders of the wild west. Yellowstone National Park has the world's highest concentration of geysers, including the tallest - Old Faithful. When driving through the west side of the park early in the morning, steam can be seen rising from the ground all around due to the boiling mud pots, vents, geysers, and hot springs.

YELLOWSTONE NATIONAL PARK
NORTHWESTERN WYOMING

DATE

FIRST REACTION

TRAVEL COMPANIONS

WEATHER CONDITIONS

ACTIVITIES

MOST MEMORABLE MOMENT

RATING

CUPS OF COFFEE

PARK   /63

MEMORABLE QUOTES

PARK STAMP

FAVORITE SPOT

DISTANCE TRAVELED

ADDITIONAL THOUGHTS

Parks

YOSEMITE | NP

Famous naturalist John Muir penned these words about this awe-inspiring national park, "No temple made with human hands can compare with Yosemite." Founded in 1890, Yosemite National Park attracts millions of visitors each year. You will want to devote more than one day to exploring the varied natural beauties of this national park. The Yosemite Valley is surrounded by towering granite wonders, 3,000 meadows, and the 5th tallest waterfall in the world. That barely scratches the surface of what this national park truly holds. Ready for an adventure? Consider taking the grueling and rewarding journey to the top of Half Dome.

YOSEMITE NATIONAL PARK
CALIFORNIA

DATE

FIRST REACTION

TRAVEL COMPANIONS

WEATHER CONDITIONS

ACTIVITIES

MOST MEMORABLE MOMENT

RATING

CUPS OF COFFEE

PARK /63

MEMORABLE QUOTES

PARK STAMP

FAVORITE SPOT

DISTANCE TRAVELED

ADDITIONAL THOUGHTS

Parks

ZION | NP

Upon arrival, you will quickly come to understand why Zion National Park was named after the Old Testament's name for Jerusalem, "Heavenly City." Located in southwestern Utah, this national park follows the Zion Canyon, which reaches depths of up to 3,000 feet and spans a distance of 15 miles. While a turn down any hiking path is sure to turn into a great adventure with beautiful sights, Zion National Park is known for two hikes in particular: The Narrows and Angels Landing. Visitors can climb to great heights along the Angels Landing Trail to see an epic view of the Zion Canyon below or can hike through the waist-deep waters of The Narrows through tall, narrow canyon walls.

ZION NATIONAL PARK
SOUTHWESTERN UTAH

DATE

FIRST REACTION

TRAVEL COMPANIONS

WEATHER CONDITIONS

ACTIVITIES

MOST MEMORABLE MOMENT

RATING

CUPS OF COFFEE

PARK /63

MEMORABLE QUOTES

PARK STAMP

FAVORITE SPOT

DISTANCE TRAVELED

ADDITIONAL THOUGHTS

112	BIG BEND
114	CARLSBAD CAVERNS
116	GRAND CANYON
118	PETRIFIED FOREST
120	SAGUARO
122	WHITE SANDS
124	GUADALUPE MOUNTAINS

Parks

BIG BEND | NP

Referred to as one of the last "wild" places in the southwest United States, Big Bend National Park is a vast, remote land full of beauty. Visitors can enjoy a variety of natural formations within the park, including vast expanses of open desert, large canyons carved by the Rio Grande River, forest-covered mountains, and even the famous "Balanced Rock." Be sure to take advantage of this unique national park by traveling down the Rio Grande River by kayak or raft or taking one of the many hikes along the canyon rim of the Rio Grande. Natural hot springs allow for relaxing finishes to long days of exploring - but communication is

BIG BEND NATIONAL PARK
SOUTHWESTERN TEXAS

DATE

FIRST REACTION

TRAVEL COMPANIONS

WEATHER CONDITIONS

ACTIVITIES

MOST MEMORABLE MOMENT

RATING

CUPS OF COFFEE

PARK /63

MEMORABLE QUOTES

PARK STAMP

FAVORITE SPOT

DISTANCE TRAVELED

ADDITIONAL THOUGHTS

Parks

CARLSBAD CAVERNS | NP

There is a lot to experience and explore at Carlsbad Caverns National Park in the Chihuahuan Desert of New Mexico. With over 119 caves and limestone rock formations, this national park has some of the longest caves around - including Lechuguilla Cave, the deepest cave in the nation. Visitors are able to explore the Carlsbad Cavern at their own pace by entering the cave through its natural entrance or by taking an elevator from the visitor center to descend into the caves below.

CARLSBAD CAVERNS NATIONAL PARK
NEW MEXICO

DATE

FIRST REACTION

TRAVEL COMPANIONS

WEATHER CONDITIONS

ACTIVITIES

MOST MEMORABLE MOMENT

RATING

CUPS OF COFFEE

PARK /63

MEMORABLE QUOTES

PARK STAMP

FAVORITE SPOT

DISTANCE TRAVELED

ADDITIONAL THOUGHTS

Parks

GRAND CANYON | NP

Attracting over 5 million visitors every year, Grand Canyon National Park is one of the nation's most beloved national parks. On a clear day, visitors can expect to see as far as 200 miles from the canyon rim. Consider experiencing the canyon from the rim or by hiking deep into the canyon for a completely different perspective. At roughly 1 mile deep and 18 miles across, hiking the Grand Canyon is not for the faint of heart! Over 90 percent of visitors view the canyon via the south rim, but the northern rim provides equally excellent views (and thinner crowds).

GRAND CANYON NATIONAL PARK
NORTHERN ARIZONA

DATE

FIRST REACTION

TRAVEL COMPANIONS

WEATHER CONDITIONS

ACTIVITIES

MOST MEMORABLE MOMENT

RATING

CUPS OF COFFEE

PARK /63

MEMORABLE QUOTES

PARK STAMP

FAVORITE SPOT

DISTANCE TRAVELED

ADDITIONAL THOUGHTS

Parks

PETRIFIED FOREST | NP

Painted badland hills and a large concentration of petrified wood in the south form the two distinctive sections of Petrified Forest National Park. These sections are some of the best-preserved areas on earth and allow visitors to catch a glimpse into prehistoric times. A majority of the hiking trails within this national park are easily accessible for any visitor. From petrified fallen trees nearly 170 feet long to tAnasazi Indian ruins upwards of 800 years old, you are sure to find sights here that are unlike anywhere else in the world.

PETRIFIED FOREST NATIONAL PARK
EASTERN ARIZONA

DATE

FIRST REACTION

TRAVEL COMPANIONS

WEATHER CONDITIONS

ACTIVITIES

MOST MEMORABLE MOMENT

RATING

CUPS OF COFFEE

PARK /63

MEMORABLE QUOTES

PARK STAMP

FAVORITE SPOT

DISTANCE TRAVELED

ADDITIONAL THOUGHTS

SAGUARO | NP

Unlike most national parks, Saguaro National Park is split into two regions, creating a Saguaro - Tuscon sandwich. With its two regions, the Tucson Mountain District in the west and the Rincon Mountain District in the east, Saguaro National Park captures the diverse beauty of the desert landscape. This national park's name came from the native saguaro cacti - with its infamous candelabra shape that stands upwards of 50 feet tall. Looking for a good spot to watch the sunset? Head to the Valley View Overlook in the Tucson Mountain District.

SAGUARO NATIONAL PARK
SOUTHERN ARIZONA

DATE

FIRST REACTION

TRAVEL COMPANIONS

WEATHER CONDITIONS

ACTIVITIES

MOST MEMORABLE MOMENT

RATING

CUPS OF COFFEE

PARK /63

MEMORABLE QUOTES

PARK STAMP

FAVORITE SPOT

DISTANCE TRAVELED

ADDITIONAL THOUGHTS

Parks

WHITE SANDS | NP

Established in 2019 as New Mexico's second national park, White Sands National Park is home to the world's largest gypsum dune field. For casual visitors, Dunes Drive is a great place to start your visit. This scenic drive will take you on a 16-mile round trip from the visitor center into the gypsum dunes. For those looking to spend more time in the park, White Sands National Park offers five different hiking trails, backcountry camping, and even sand sledding. If you forgot to bring your sled to New Mexico, you could easily purchase or rent one at the visitor center.

WHITE SANDS NATIONAL PARK
NEW MEXICO

DATE

FIRST REACTION

TRAVEL COMPANIONS

WEATHER CONDITIONS

ACTIVITIES

MOST MEMORABLE MOMENT

RATING

CUPS OF COFFEE

PARK
/63

MEMORABLE QUOTES

PARK STAMP

FAVORITE SPOT

DISTANCE TRAVELED

ADDITIONAL THOUGHTS

Parks

GUADALUPE MOUNTAINS | NP

Guadalupe Mountains National Park is located near the New Mexico border in western Texas. This park is home to the tallest mountain peaks in Texas, surrounded by diverse plant and animal life. The dry mountains stand in contrast to the greenery around them, which turns to vibrant colors in the spring and fall. Popular activities in this national park include climbing Guadalupe Peak, visiting the Salt Basin Dunes, and hiking the Devil's Hall Trail.

GUADALUPE MOUNTAINS NATIONAL PARK
WESTERN TEXAS

DATE

FIRST REACTION

TRAVEL COMPANIONS

WEATHER CONDITIONS

ACTIVITIES

MOST MEMORABLE MOMENT

RATING

CUPS OF COFFEE

PARK /63

MEMORABLE QUOTES

PARK STAMP

FAVORITE SPOT

DISTANCE TRAVELED

ADDITIONAL THOUGHTS

THE BEAUTIFUL NAT'L PARKS OF

Hawaii
ALASKA

128	DENALI
130	GATES OF THE ARCTIC
132	GLACIER BAY
134	HALEAKALA
136	HAWAII VOLCANOES
138	KATMAI
140	KENAI FJORDS
142	KOBUK VALLEY
144	LAKE CLARK
146	WRANGELL ST. ELIAS

Parks

DENALI | NP

Denali National Park is home to Denali, the highest mountain peak in North America. Formerly known as Mt. McKinley, this 20,310-foot wonder overlooks the beautiful Alaskan landscape and the caribou, grizzly bears, wolves, and Dall sheep that fill it. Drive through this park via the 85-mile Park Road on a summer day - or night - for that matter. During the summer months, expect days with up to 24 hours of sunlight, but visiting between August and April will give you the best chance to see the stunning northern lights.

DENALI NATIONAL PARK
ALASKA

DATE

FIRST REACTION

TRAVEL COMPANIONS

WEATHER CONDITIONS

ACTIVITIES

MOST MEMORABLE MOMENT

RATING

CUPS OF COFFEE

PARK /63

MEMORABLE QUOTES

PARK STAMP

FAVORITE SPOT

DISTANCE TRAVELED

ADDITIONAL THOUGHTS

Parks

GATES OF THE ARCTIC | NP

Accessible only by plane, Gates of the Arctic National Park boasts a whopping 8,472,506 acres of wilderness. Within this Alaskan wilderness are six wild rivers, countless jagged granite peaks, and dozens of beautiful mountain lakes. This landscape is perfect for hikers, fishers, and backpackers looking for solitude in one of the last true wildernesses in the United States. Due to the remote nature of this park, Gates of the Arctic National Park is the least visited national park in the United States. National park passport stamps are available outside of the park at the Bettles Visitor Center and the Arctic Interagency Visitor Center in Coldfoot.

GATES OF THE ARCTIC NATIONAL PARK
NORHTERN ALASKA

DATE | FIRST REACTION

TRAVEL COMPANIONS

WEATHER CONDITIONS

ACTIVITIES

MOST MEMORABLE MOMENT

RATING | CUPS OF COFFEE | PARK /63

MEMORABLE QUOTES | PARK STAMP

FAVORITE SPOT

DISTANCE TRAVELED

ADDITIONAL THOUGHTS

Parks

GLACIER BAY | NP

Nearly 250 years ago, the gorgeous Alaskan land now known as Glacier Bay National Park was covered by a thick glacier. This glacier retreated 65 miles and exposed this land that is now full of plant and animal life. This national park is accessible only by boat or plane, and many choose to access it by cruise ship or by sea kayak. Stop by the Huna Tribal House, built as a symbol of peace between the Huna Tlingit people and the National Park Service, or create an adventure yourself by hiking, mountaineering, sea kayaking, or even rafting.

GLACIER BAY NATIONAL PARK
SOUTHEASTERN ALASKA

DATE | FIRST REACTION

TRAVEL COMPANIONS

WEATHER CONDITIONS

ACTIVITIES

MOST MEMORABLE MOMENT

RATING | CUPS OF COFFEE | PARK
　　　　　　　　　　　　　　　　　　/63

MEMORABLE QUOTES | PARK STAMP

FAVORITE SPOT

DISTANCE TRAVELED

ADDITIONAL THOUGHTS

Parks

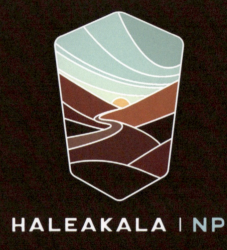

HALEAKALA | NP

Towering 10,023 ft. above the fluorescent-blue waters of the Maui coast lies the crown of Haleakala National Park: the Haleakala Crater. This dormant volcano, known in the traditional Hawaiian language as the "House of the Sun," is known for its brilliant sunrise view. Don't be fooled, however. Even on this tropical island, a jacket is a must at such a high altitude. Haleakala National Park has many more areas to explore if climbing to the top of a volcano doesn't pique your interest. Mars-red deserts, waterfalls, and an abundance of hiking trails make Haleakala a destination for adventurers.

HALEAKALA NATIONAL PARK
MAUI, HAWAI'I

DATE

FIRST REACTION

TRAVEL COMPANIONS

WEATHER CONDITIONS

ACTIVITIES

MOST MEMORABLE MOMENT

RATING

CUPS OF COFFEE

PARK   /63

MEMORABLE QUOTES

PARK STAMP

FAVORITE SPOT

DISTANCE TRAVELED

ADDITIONAL THOUGHTS

Parks

HAWAII VOLCANOES | NP

Located on the "Big Island," Hawai'i Volcanoes National Park is home to the world's two most active volcanoes: Kīlauea and Mauna Loa. The landscape of this park is constantly changing and even grew by 875 acres in 1983. This uncontrollable power of nature has proven extremely dangerous but provides magnificent views to visitors brave enough to make the trip. Expect to see numerous cinder cones, lava tubes, craters, and potentially molten lava if you're "lucky."

HAWAI'I VOLCANOES NATIONAL PARK
HAWAI'I

DATE

FIRST REACTION

TRAVEL COMPANIONS

WEATHER CONDITIONS

ACTIVITIES

MOST MEMORABLE MOMENT

RATING

CUPS OF COFFEE

PARK /63

MEMORABLE QUOTES

PARK STAMP

FAVORITE SPOT

DISTANCE TRAVELED

ADDITIONAL THOUGHTS

Parks

KATMAI | NP

Katmai National Park went from "unknown" to "known" when a powerful volcanic eruption from a volcano cooled air temperatures around the world in 1912. This national park contains at least 14 active volcanoes and an estimated 2,200 brown bears. Accessible only by plane or boat, explorers have many opportunities for adventures via water or air when they enter the Katmai wilderness.

KATMAI NATIONAL PARK
SOUTHERN ALASKA

DATE

FIRST REACTION

TRAVEL COMPANIONS

WEATHER CONDITIONS

ACTIVITIES

MOST MEMORABLE MOMENT

RATING

CUPS OF COFFEE

PARK /63

MEMORABLE QUOTES

PARK STAMP

FAVORITE SPOT

DISTANCE TRAVELED

ADDITIONAL THOUGHTS

Parks

KENAI FJORDS | NP

Although Kenai Fjords National Park is the smallest of Alaska's national parks, it is breathtaking and filled with as many varied landscapes and wildlife as any other. This national park is accessible by car, and visitors can take the incredibly scenic 130-mile road from Anchorage to Seward to begin their journey. Visitors can then hike along the Harding Icefield Trail, take a boating tour of the fjords, or look for wildlife along the Nuka River.

KENAI FJORDS NATIONAL PARK
SOUTHERN ALASKA

DATE

FIRST REACTION

TRAVEL COMPANIONS

WEATHER CONDITIONS

ACTIVITIES

MOST MEMORABLE MOMENT

RATING

CUPS OF COFFEE

PARK   /63

MEMORABLE QUOTES

PARK STAMP

FAVORITE SPOT

DISTANCE TRAVELED

ADDITIONAL THOUGHTS

Parks

KOBUK VALLEY | NP

The entirety of this remote national park is located above the Arctic Circle, which is part of the reason it is one of the least visited national parks. Despite its difficult accessibility, Kobuk Valley National Park has quite a unique landscape. Mountains and a spruce forest surround the sweeping sand dunes nestled in this valley. Accessible only by plane, Kobuk Valley National Park is explored best by using a combination of walking and boating, as the Kobuk River cuts through this beautiful valley.

KOBUK VALLEY NATIONAL PARK
NORTHERN ALASKA

DATE

FIRST REACTION

TRAVEL COMPANIONS

WEATHER CONDITIONS

ACTIVITIES

MOST MEMORABLE MOMENT

RATING

CUPS OF COFFEE

PARK /63

MEMORABLE QUOTES

PARK STAMP

FAVORITE SPOT

DISTANCE TRAVELED

ADDITIONAL THOUGHTS

Parks

LAKE CLARK | NP

Lake Clark National Park is full of stunning lakes, towering mountain ranges, steaming volcanoes, and a wide variety of wildlife. To access this Alaskan national park, visitors must fly deep into the park or take a boat to the coast. Many visitors are drawn here by the incredible opportunities for fishing, and others come to backpack, hike, kayak, or birdwatch. Does this picture look familiar? Close the book, and you'll see what we mean.

LAKE CLARK NATIONAL PARK
ALASKA

DATE

FIRST REACTION

TRAVEL COMPANIONS

WEATHER CONDITIONS

ACTIVITIES

MOST MEMORABLE MOMENT

RATING

CUPS OF COFFEE

PARK /63

MEMORABLE QUOTES

PARK STAMP

FAVORITE SPOT

DISTANCE TRAVELED

ADDITIONAL THOUGHTS

Parks

WRANGELL ST. ELIAS | NP

13,188,000 acres. Let that number sink in. Wrangell - St. Elias National Park is by far the largest national park - nearly double the size of the State of Massachusetts. This national park is accessible by plane or car, and visiting in the summer months allows visitors to see more of this beautiful landscape. Its three mountain ranges hold 9 of the 16 tallest mountains in the United States. Be sure and do your research before heading here – there are plenty of wilderness adventures awaiting your arrival.

WRANGELL ST. ELIAS NATIONAL PARK
SOUTHEASTERN ALASKA

DATE | FIRST REACTION

TRAVEL COMPANIONS

WEATHER CONDITIONS

ACTIVITIES

MOST MEMORABLE MOMENT

RATING | CUPS OF COFFEE | PARK /63

MEMORABLE QUOTES | PARK STAMP

FAVORITE SPOT

DISTANCE TRAVELED

ADDITIONAL THOUGHTS

150	AMERICAN SAMOA
152	U.S. VIRGIN ISLANDS

Parks

NATIONAL PARK OF
AMERICAN SAMOA

The National Park of American Samoa is a place overflowing with tropical beauty. American Samoa is recognized as a United States territory and sits in the Pacific Ocean about 2,500 miles southwest of Hawaii. The Samoan people work hard to care for Samoa - a word that means "sacred earth." The National Park of American Samoa is comprised of five islands and two coral atolls that are brimming with diverse plant and animal life. Visitors can expect this national park to be hot and rainy regardless of the time of year, as these islands rest close to the Equator.

NATIONAL PARK OF AMERICAN SAMOA
AMERICAN SAMOA

DATE

FIRST REACTION

TRAVEL COMPANIONS

WEATHER CONDITIONS

ACTIVITIES

MOST MEMORABLE MOMENT

RATING

CUPS OF COFFEE

PARK /63

MEMORABLE QUOTES

PARK STAMP

FAVORITE SPOT

DISTANCE TRAVELED

ADDITIONAL THOUGHTS

Parks

VIRGIN ISLANDS | NP

Located on the Island of St. John, Virgin Islands National Park is a beautiful Caribbean destination full of history, beaches, tropical forests, and aquatic life. You will find no shortage of excursions to take while at Virgin Islands National Park. World-class snorkeling, hiking trails that lead to historical jungle ruins, and some of the most pristine beaches on earth are just a few popular selling points. Due to the unique history of this national park, you will also find many non-native wildlife species like burros, sheep, deer, goats, and pigs. You may even find some of them taking a swim in the ocean to cool off in the heat of the afternoon!

VIRGIN ISLANDS NATIONAL PARK
U.S. VIRGIN ISLANDS

DATE

FIRST REACTION

TRAVEL COMPANIONS

WEATHER CONDITIONS

ACTIVITIES

MOST MEMORABLE MOMENT

RATING

CUPS OF COFFEE

PARK /63

MEMORABLE QUOTES

PARK STAMP

FAVORITE SPOT

DISTANCE TRAVELED

ADDITIONAL THOUGHTS

NOTES

NOTES

NOTES

NOTES

Copyright © 2022 Flatlander Trading

All rights reserved. No part of this book may be scanned, uploaded, reproduced, or used in any manner without the prior written permission of the copyright owner, except for the use of brief quotations in a book review.

To request permissions, contact Flatlander Trading at www.flatlandertrading.com

ISBN 979-8-218-00000-4

Second Edition

Cover art by Jesse Balmer
Layout by Jesse Balmer
Illustrated by Jesse Balmer
Research and text by Samuel Stevens
Research and text by Dylan Balmer

Printed in the USA.

Your Passport to the Parks was not designed to serve as a travel guide, a history book, or a to-do list for your adventures. We understand that there are a plethora of ways that people gather information to inform their travels, and we are not seeking to replace those methods that are tried and true. We highly encourage you to seek up-to-date information about parks before you visit, as conditions and regulations are always changing.

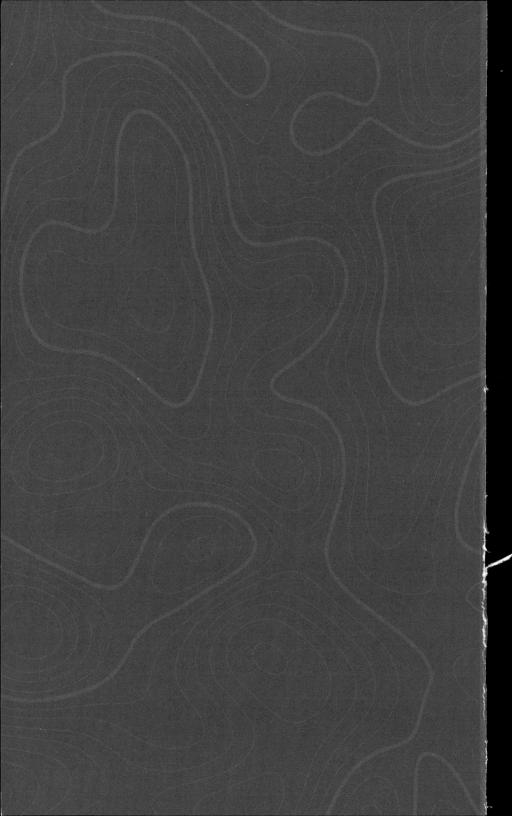